this day in Sports

By John G. Fetros

A DIARY OF
MAJOR SPORTS EVENTS

NEWTON K. GREGG / PUBLISHER

NOVATO, CALIFORNIA

ISBN 0-912318-58-9
Library of Congress Catalog Card Number 74-75882
Copyright © 1974 By John Fetros
Printed in the United States of America

INTRODUCTION

Sports events are no longer tucked away in the sports pages, isolated from the mainstream of human events. They have moved up to the front page. Think of Mark Spitz' incredible medal-collecting at the Olympics and its tragic counterpoint — the assassination of members of the Israeli team; the tense drama of Hank Aaron's challenge to home run records; the ping-pong diplomacy that helped reopen contact between the U.S. and China; women's liberation fought out on the tennis court by Bobby Riggs and Billy Jean King; or the Fischer-Spassky chess match in Iceland that was watched by the entire world. These events go beyond sport to human drama, international and sexual politics, racial problems, space-age communications, and changing social patterns that involve and affect us all.

As sports become a more and more integral part of our lives, sports facts from today, the 20's or from the 18th century become more than interesting reading. They become a lively document of social change, a fascinating connection with the past.

And scanning back over sports headlines, you often discover an uncanny relevance to the 1970's. You'll feel a shiver of recognition, in this book, as you hear a UCLA sports professor urge, in 1944, that sports not be given up because of the gasoline shortage; sportswriters discredit the triumph, in 1933, of the world's greatest woman tennis player Helen Wills Moody over a male player; or the *Harvard Crimson* asking, in 1931, that Army be eliminated from the Harvard football schedule because of the alienation of Harvard men from the U.S. military machine.

Brief and concise, with emphasis on major and minor sports of greatest current interest to Americans, this calendar of sports history has a wide appeal and a broad spectrum of uses.

The sports writer or announcer on radio or television will find fascinating filler data, and ideas for longer treatment in feature articles or columns.

The teacher will find topics for assignments, themes to provoke class discussion, and a way of involving children bored by the traditional approach to history.

Speakers at sports banquets will draw from the book a rich and amusing range of material to incorporate into their speeches.

Sporting goods stores might glean colorful ideas for displays and sales promotions.

Librarians will find it invaluable as a basic reference work.

And sports buffs of all ages will use it constantly to satisfy their voracious appetite for facts.

But for everyone, THIS DAY IN SPORTS will be far more than a useful list of statistics, or a valuable and durable record of great names and events. It will be a fresh perspective on ourselves, and on our history.

* * * * * *

JANUARY 1

1767   The first American fox hunting club, the Gloucester Fox Hunting Club near Philadelphia, begins its activities.

1840   The first American bowling tournament match recorded is held in New York at the Knickerbocker Alleys.

1856   Timothy Keefe, baseball player, pitcher of a record nineteen consecutive wins in 1883, Baseball Hall of Fame member, born.

1862   Baron Pierre de Coubertin, French educator and sportsman whose efforts revived the Olympic Games in modern times, born.

1890   The first Tournament of Roses which featured amateur sports contests is held in Pasadena, California.

1897   The first football game between Negro colleges is held in Atlanta, Georgia between Atlanta University and Tuskegee Normal and Industrial Institute with Atlanta winning 10-0.

1902   The first Tournament of Roses college football game is held in Pasadena, California as the University of Michigan defeats Stanford 49-0 so decisively that no other Rose Bowl is played for fourteen years.

1904   Ethan Allen, baseball player, born.

1911   Henry (Hank) Greenberg, Baseball Hall of Fame member, the American League Most Valuable Player in 1935 and 1940, born.

1916   The first of the permanent annual Rose Bowl football games is held as Washington State College defeats Brown University 14-0.

1921   John Logan, basketball player, born.

1921   California defeats Ohio State 28-0 in the Rose Bowl in a game which saw Brick Muller of California throw a pass some estimate as being 70 yards.

1924   Clifford Earl Torgeson, baseball player, born.

1925   Notre Dame's "Four Horsemen" play together for the last time as their team defeats Stanford 27-10 in the Rose Bowl.

1926   Alabama, the first Southern team to play in the Rose Bowl, defeats Washington 20-19 in a game that serves as a stepping stone for Johnny Mack Brown to become a movie star.

1927   Ewell Doak Walker, Jr., football player, selected on practically every All-American team in 1947 and 1948, Maxwell Award winner in 1947, Heisman winner in 1948, *Sport Magazine* 1948 Outstanding College Player, born.

1929   The Prarie View Bowl game, the first Negro college football bowl game, is played in Houston, Texas with Prarie View losing 6-0 to Atlanta University.

1929   Roy Riegels runs sixty-nine yards the wrong way in a Rose Bowl game between Georgia Tech and California which Georgia Tech wins 8-7.

1934   Columbia upsets Stanford 7-0 in the Rose Bowl in a game witnessed by Stanford alumnus President Hoover.

1935   Tulane defeats Temple in the first Sugar Bowl game 20-14, at New Orleans, Louisiana.

1936   The first Sun Bowl is played with Hardin Simmons University tying New Mexico State 14-14, at El Paso, Texas.

1937   The first Cotton Bowl is played, at Dallas, Texas, with Texas Christian University defeating Marquette 16-6.

5

1938   The Eastern College Athletic Conference, the largest collegiate athletic conference in the nation, begins operations as the Central Office for Eastern Intercollegiate Athletics.

1940   Marlin McKeever, football player, born.

1945   Bob Waterfield wins the first William M. Coffman Trophy as the outstanding game player for leading the West to a 13-7 win over the East in the East-West football game in San Francisco, California.

1946   The first Gator Bowl is played, in Jacksonville, Florida, with Wake Forest defeating South Carolina 26-14.

1947   Claude (Buddy) Young of the University of Illinois becomes the first Negro to score a Rose Bowl touchdown as Illinois defeats UCLA 45-14.

1951   Kentucky upsets Oklahoma in the Sugar Bowl at New Orleans 13-7 to end Oklahoma's thirty-one game winning streak.

1951   In horse racing, Bolero wins the San Carlos Handicap at Santa Anita race track in Arcadia, California in world record time of 1 minute, 21 seconds for the seven furlongs.

1952   The first Negro marching unit participated in the Rose Bowl parade in Pasadena, California.

1955   Charley Bryant and Jon McWilliams of Nebraska become the first Negroes to play in the Orange Bowl at Miami, Florida as their team is defeated by Duke 34-7.

1967   The Green Bay Packers defeat the Dallas Cowboys 34-27 for the National Football League championship and the right to represent the National Football League in the first Super Bowl.

JANUARY 2

1870   George (Tex) Rickard, fight promoter of the Dempsey-Carpentier and the second Dempsey-Tunney fights, born.

1894   Arthur Nielsen, tennis philantropist, born.

1915   Duke Kahanamoku sets a world record in swimming the 100 yards in 53.8 seconds.

1920   Bob Feerick, basketball player, born.

1937   Martin Lauer, German hurdler, the 1959 *Track and Field News* World Athlete of the Year, born.

1940   Patrick Fischer, football player, born.

1945   Horse racing in the United States ends in compliance with the Federal Government's wartime conservation order.

1947   Calvin Hill, *The Sporting News* National Football League Rookie of the Year in 1969, born.

1947   City College of New York bars any team coached by Everett Shelton from competition with CCNY teams because of allegedly anti-Semitic remarks made by Shelton during a basketball game in which CCNY beat Shelton's Wyoming University team.

1957   Gene Fullmer wins the world middleweight title from Sugar Ray Robinson.

1960   Bobby Fischer successfully defends his United States chess championship in a New York tournament.

1961   Bobby Fischer wins his fourth consecutive United States chess championship in New York by drawing with the Hungarian grandmaster Pal Benko.

1965 Joe Namath signs a $400,000 contract with the New York Jets becoming the richest rookie in professional football history.

1968 Sugar Ray Robinson is elected to the boxing Hall of Fame.

1969 Max Baer is elected to the boxing Hall of Fame.

1970 Edgar Diddle, basketball coach of Western Kentucky University from 1922 to 1964, died.

JANUARY 3

1924 Hank Stram, football coach, born.

1939 Bobby Hull, hockey player, Hart Trophy winner for Most Valuable Player in the National Hockey League in 1965 and 1966, Lady Byng Trophy winner for Sportsmanship in 1965, born.

1939 16,000 fans turn out at Madison Square Garden in New York to see Don Budge make his professional tennis debut.

1940 Adios, the standardbred stallion who was the most influential sire of any breed of livestock in America in modern times, is foaled at Carmel, Indiana.

1941 The National Collegiate Football Rules Committee adopts a rule change permitting the substitution of players as many times as desired.

1942 The East-West football game is played at New Orleans, Louisiana due to the war and ends in a 6-6 tie, a game that sees ten of Grantland Rice's eleven All-Americans on the squads.

1951 Fred Wilt, track star, wins the Amateur Athletic Union's Sullivan Memorial Trophy as the top United States amateur athlete of 1950.

1954 A professional tennis troupe of Frank Sedgman, Richard (Pancho) Gonzales, Francisco (Pancho) Segura, Donald Budge, and Jack Kramer begin a nationwide tour.

1972 Nebraska receives all fifty-five first place votes and is selected by the Associated Press as the top collegiate football team in the country with Oklahoma and Colorado, also Big Eight Conference teams, second and third, the first time since 1936 that three teams from the same conference had swept the top rankings.

1973 The New York Yankees baseball team is sold by the Columbia Broadcasting System to a twelve man syndicate for $10,000,000.

JANUARY 4

1850 The first American ice skating club, the Skaters' Club of the City and County of Philadelphia, is organized in Philadelphia, Pennsylvania.

1887 Pat Ryan, 1920 Olympic hammer throw champion, born.

1887   The first bicycle trip around the world is completed in San Francisco, California by Thomas Stevens who had started the trip April 22, 1884 from San Francisco.

1925   John Lujack, football player, 1947 Heisman Trophy winner as the country's outstanding football player, in 1944 Notre Dame's first four letter athlete in a quarter century, born.

1930   Don Shula, football coach, born.

1935   Floyd Patterson, heavyweight boxing champion of the world, born.

1941   Kermit Alexander, football player, born.

1943   Bobby Burnett, football player, *The Sporting News* 1966 American Football League Rookie of the Year, born.

1945   Ann Curtis, holder of eight national AAU swimming titles, is announced as the first woman to receive the James E. Sullivan Memorial Trophy.

1946   George Woolf, Jockey Hall of Fame member, leading jockey in number of stakes victories in 1942 and 1944, died after being thrown to the ground by a horse during a race at Santa Anita race track in Arcadia, California.

1947   George (Butch) Atkinson, football player, born.

1947   British speed driver Donald Campbell, former world speed record holder for both land and water, is killed when his speedboat is destroyed on Coniston Lake in northwest England.

1968   The United Soccer Association and the National Professional Soccer League announce a merger into a new two division Professional Soccer League.

JANUARY 5

1864   Byron (Ban) Johnson, originator of the "Cincinnati Agreement" of 1903 which established two major leagues in baseball, Baseball Hall of Fame member, born.

1932   Chuck Noll, football coach, born.

1934   The National and American Leagues select a uniform ball to be used by both leagues, the first time in thirty-three years both leagues will use the same baseball.

1938   James Otto, football player, born.

1941   Charles (Chuck) McKinley, tennis player, winner of the 1963 Wimbledon men's singles title, the first American to win this since 1955, United States men's singles indoor champion in 1962 and 1964, born.

1942   The University of Oklahoma formally protests as prejudicial, unfair and arbitrary the action of the Big Six eligibility committee which disqualified Gerald Tucker, a star Oklahoma basketball player, as a migrant athlete.

1949   A match race is held at Tropical Park in Coral Gables, Florida between the quarter horse champion, Stella Moore, and the thoroughbred race horse Olympia with Olympia winning the race which was run at a distance of 73 feet short of a quarter mile.

1951   St. Mary's College of Oakland, California dropped intercollegiate football for the duration of the national emergency.

1957   Pat McCormick, Olympic diving champion, is designated by an Associated Press poll of sportswriters and sportscasters to receive the Babe Didrikson Zaharias Trophy as the outstanding United States female athlete of 1956.

1963   Rogers Hornsby, Baseball Hall of Fame member with a lifetime batting average of .358 topped only by Ty Cobb's, died.

1963   Jim Beatty of Los Angeles, California, the first man to run an under four minute mile indoors, is named winner of the James E. Sullivan Memorial Trophy as 1962's outstanding amateur athlete.

JANUARY 6

1896   The first American women's six day bicycle race begins at Madison Square Garden in New York.

1919   Roy Cochran, Olympic gold medal winner in the low hurdles in 1948, born.

1920   Early Wynn, baseball pitcher who won over three hundred games, Cy Young Award winner in 1959, born.

1921   Cary Middlecoff, golfer, 1955 Masters winner, born.

1925   Paavo Nurmi, the "Flying Ghost of Finland" running on boards for the first time, breaks two world records in ninety minutes with a new indoor mile time of 4 minutes, 13 3/5 seconds and a new 5,000-meter time of 14 minutes, 44 3/5 seconds at the Finnish-American track meet at Madison Square Garden in New York.

1926   Ralph Branca, baseball player, born.

1930   The French Lawn Tennis Federation considers protest against a propaganda tour of French tennis champions led by Henri Cochet to Japan, Egypt, and India on the grounds it imperiled amateurism since French sports writers questioned how an amateur could afford five months of constant travel.

1931   Richard (Dickie) Moore, hockey player, Ross Trophy winner, born.

1932   Joie Ray, former track star, competes in a dance marathon in Newark, New Jersey stating he couldn't live on medals or even sell them and had tried roller skating, racing against a horse, and prize fighting to make ends meet.

1933   Leonard Green, baseball player, born.

1936   Darlene Hard, top ranked female tennis player in 1962, national women's singles title holder in 1960 and 1961, born.

1940   Ed Barrow of the New York Yankees states that regardless of legislation against the Yankees restricting their ability to trade they would not respond to pleas to help the St. Louis Browns and other weak teams and that all surplus players would be directed outside the league.

1941   Alice Marble, world's champion woman tennis player, makes her professional debut defeating Ruth Hardwick of Great Britain at Madison Square Garden in New York.

1942   The National Collegiate Football Rules Committee abolishes the Y formation in which the center faces his backfield.

1954   Volomite, the world's foremost standardbred sire, died at the age of twenty-eight.

JANUARY 7

1869   The Amateur Swimming Association, governing body for the sport in England, is formed.

1890   Maurice Evans McLoughlin, Tennis Hall of Fame member known as "The California Comet," born.

1897   The first national handball championship match for amateurs begins at Jersey City, New Jersey with the first winner being Michael Eagan.

1922   Alvin Dark, baseball player and manager, the 1948 Rookie of the Year, born.

1930   Edward Le Baron, Jr., football player, born.

1943   James Lefebvre, baseball player, 1965 National League Rookie of the Year, born.

1945   Anthony Conigliaro, baseball player, born.

1950   The first Senior Bowl football game for North and South all-star teams of college seniors is held, in Jacksonville, Florida, with the South winning over the North 22-13.

1959   The Harlem Globetrotters basketball team celebrate the thirty-second anniversary of their first playing date, at Melbourne, Australia.

1960   The California State Athletic Commission withdrew from the National Boxing Association on grounds the National Boxing Association had failed to develop an effective national regulation to eliminate hoodlum influence from boxing.

1961   Detroit defeats Cleveland 17-16 in the inaugural Playoff Bowl between second place teams in each conference of the National Football League.

1968   Fred Anton Maier of Norway set a world 5,000-meter speedskating record of 7 minutes, 26.2 seconds in Deventer, The Netherlands.

JANUARY 8

1901   The first bowling tournament sponsored by the American Bowling Congress convenes, at Chicago, Illinois.

1915   William Walker Cooper, baseball player sold by the St. Louis Cardinals to the New York Giants for $175,000 in 1946 while he was in the Navy, born.

1925   Wayne (Big) Munn, former Nebraska University football star, defeats Ed (Strangler) Lewis before 15,000 fans in Kansas City, Missouri and claims the wrestling championship of the world.

1932   Williamette University of Salem, Oregon denies charges in a suit filed by Harold McKenzie, former football guard, that he had been hired for $75 a month in cash, $10 a month during the school year and

10

a passing grade in hygiene in return for becoming a member of the University football team.

1940   Al Hostak, in Chicago for a fight with Tony Zale, lets his brother speak for him in a sports broadcast over a local station because of his superstition it was bad luck to speak over the radio before a fight.

1954   Dr. Wallace Howell's rainmaking firm was employed by ski resort operators in Vermont to try to relieve a shortage of snow in the area.

1955   Georgia Tech defeated Kentucky's basketball team 59-58, Kentucky's first loss since January 2, 1943 in one hundred thirty home basketball games.

1957   Jackie Robinson announces in a *Look* article his retirement from baseball to become a vice president of Chock-Full-O'Nuts.

1960   The National Collegiate Athletic Association convention in New York voted against reviving the unlimited substitution rule in college football.

1963   Jacob (Jack) Molinas was convicted as the master fixer in a basketball bribery scandal that involved forty-seven players from twenty-seven colleges.

1972   The National Collegiate Athletic Association votes to give major colleges permission to let freshman play varsity football and basketball expanding a previous 1969 ruling allowing varsity status in other sports at major colleges and allowing major schools the same basketball-football programs as small schools.

JANUARY 9

1793   The first United States free flight in a balloon is made at Philadelphia, Pennsylvania by Jean Pierre Blanchard in an event witnessed by a large crowd that includes George Washington.

1910   A notice in *The Dartmouth* results in the formation of the Outing Club and the start of Dartmouth's Winter Carnival.

1934   Bryan (Bart) Starr, football player, *The Sporting News* National Football League Player of the Year in 1966, born.

1936   Ralph Terry, baseball player, born.

1942   In his twentieth defense of his world heavyweight title, Joe Louis knocks out Buddy Baer in the first round.

1948   The Executive Committee of the United States Golf Association decides to inaugurate a junior amateur golf championship for boys who had not reached their eighteenth birthday.

1951   Samuel D. Riddle, owner of Man o'War, died.

1951   Australia clinched "The Ashes" trophy, the mythical world cricket title, defeating England, in Sydney, Australia, thus retaining the title it had held since 1932.

1968   The National Collegiate Athletic Association named former Massachusetts Senator Leverett Saltonstall as recipient of its Theodore Roosevelt Award given to a man who was a varsity athlete in college and who later became a leading citizen.

JANUARY 10

1915 Great Britain and Canada cancel major golf tournaments because of the war.

1930 Dan Ferris, secretary of the Amateur Athletic Union, says the Olympic Games of 1932 in Los Angeles will give a surer test of international supremacy because only about thirty nations will be represented as opposed to forty-five in the 1928 Games thus reducing the number of preliminary heats needed.

1938 Francis (Frank) Mahovlich, hockey player, Calder Trophy winner, born.

1939 William Toomey, the 1968 Olympic decathlon winner, born.

1942 The United States Golf Association cancels the open, the amateur, the women's amateur and the amateur public links championships for 1942 because of the war.

1948 The National Collegiate Athletic Association adopted its "sanity code" against special leniency for athletes in granting scholarships or sports professionalism in NCAA colleges.

1949 George Foreman, world heavyweight boxing champion, born.

1950 Ben Hogan tied Sam Snead for first place in the Los Angeles Open in his first golf tournament appearance since his automobile accident in 1949 but he loses the title in a playoff.

1955 Squaw Valley, California is approved by the United States Olympic Committee for recommendation as the site of the 1960 Olympic Winter Games.

1963 Robert Whitlow, Air Force Academy athletic director and a retiring Air Force colonel, was named as athletic director of the National League's Chicago Cubs, the first such post in major league baseball.

JANUARY 11

1911 Jack (Jumping Jack) McCracken, basketball player, Basketball Hall of Fame member, born.

1922 Cornelius John Berry, baseball player, born.

1942 George Mira, football player, 1963 major college total offense leader, born.

1947 Honus Wagner signs his thirty-sixth major league baseball contract in Pittsburgh signing as a Pirate coach.

1948 Madeline Manning, track star, born.

1949 After winning the Los Angeles Open golf tournament, Lloyd Mangrum credits his win to a change of equipment and to a lucky pair of pajamas he wore under his pants.

1957 The National Collegiate Athletic Association adopted a rule to limit an athlete's financial help from all sources when based partly on athletic ability to commonly accepted educational expenses.

1964 Charles (Bud) Wilkinson, head football coach of the University of Oklahoma for seventeen years, resigns.

1964 Wendell Mottley tied the world indoor record for the 500-yard run with a time of 55.5 seconds, in track competition at Boston, Massachusetts.

1965   The National Football League Pro Bowl is shifted from New Orleans to Houston when twenty-one Negro players claim discrimination by New Orleans' night clubs and taxi drivers.

1970   Billy Casper became the second professional golfer to reach the $1,000,000 mark in earnings by winning a playoff in the Los Angeles Open.

1970   The Kansas City Chiefs defeated the Minnesota Vikings 27-7 to win the United States professional football championship.

1973   The owners of the twenty-four major league baseball teams voted to allow the American League to experiment with a tenth player, the "designated hitter' who could bat for a pitcher without forcing him out of the game, during the next three seasons.

JANUARY 12

1879   Ray Harroun, auto racer, winner in 1911 of the first Indianapolis 500 race, born.

1895   Alvin (Bo) McMillin, All-American football player, National Football Foundation Hall of Fame member, coach, born.

1899   Herbert Orrin (Fritz) Crisler, football coach at Minnesota, Princeton, and Michigan, College Football Coach of the Year in 1947, born.

1906   The American Inter-Collegiate Football Rules Committee adopts a reform to make games safe by legalizing the forward pass.

1907   The Missouri Valley Conference of colleges and universities is formed in Kansas City, Missouri.

1912   Georgia Coleman, the American swimming star who was the first woman to do a 2 1/2 forward somersault in competition, winner of the Olympic diving gold medal for women in 1932 in the fancy springboard dive category, born.

1921   Judge Kenesaw Mountain Landis takes office as baseball commissioner.

1928   Lloyd Ruby, auto racer, born.

1943   Ivan (Tucker) Frederickson, football player, born.

1944   Joe Frazier, heavyweight boxing champion, born.

1946   The National Football League transfers the franchise and Cleveland Rams club to Los Angeles, California.

1952   Terry Browne, ice skating champion, sets a world barrel jumping distance record of 28 feet, 3 inches, clearing fifteen barrels in Grossinger, New York to retain the World Barrel Jumping Championship.

1957   Murray Rose of Australia breaks world records in swimming the 440-yard freestyle in 4 minutes, 27.1 seconds and the 400-meter freestyle in 4 minutes, 25.9 seconds.

1960   Dolph Schayes of the Syracuse professional basketball team becomes the first professional basketball player to score more than 15,000 points by finishing a game against the Boston Celtics at Philadelphia with a record 15,013 points.

1961 Chicago Cubs president Phil Wrigley announced that for the 1961 season a staff of eight coaches would manage the baseball team instead of a team manager.

1969 Charles Sifford wins the Los Angeles Open golf tournament in a sudden death playoff becoming the second Negro to win a major professional golf tournament.

1969 The New York Jets score a 16-7 upset over the Baltimore Colts giving the American Football League its first major triumph over the National Football League and its first Super Bowl victory.

JANUARY 13

1886 A.H. Rose, inventor of the net and puck used in the National Hockey League, Hockey Hall of Fame member for whom the Art Ross Trophy for highest point total of goals and assists is named, born.

1933 Tom Gola, basketball player, born.

1933 Mildred (Babe) Didrikson makes her first professional basketball appearance scoring nine points as her team, the Brooklyn Yankees, defeats the Long Island Ducklings 19-16 in a game played in New York.

1938 The All-America Redheads, a women's basketball team from Missouri which has four girls on its team over six feet tall, meets a team of men from Warner Brothers Studios, in Los Angeles at the Pan Pacific Auditorium, refusing any modification of rules because of the fact they are women.

1939 The Eastern Intercollegiate Baseball League decided the yellow ball may be used in college games if competing teams agree.

1939 Monty Stratton whose right leg was amputated after a hunting accident is listed among the thirty-two players on the 1939 roster of the Chicago White Sox after he indicated he is determined to pitch with the aid of his artificial leg.

1939 The *New York Herald Tribune* reveals Samuel D. Riddle had been offered one million dollars for his race horse Man o'War by Louis B. Mayer, a surprising figure since Man o'War was twenty-two years old and had a reduced stud value.

1950 George Widener is elected chairman of the Jockey Club succeeding William Woodward.

1951 Your Host suffers a broken leg in a spill during the running of the San Pasqual Handicap at Santa Anita race track in Arcadia, California and his racing career is ended.

1962 The National Collegiate Athletic Association votes unanimously to support the creation of new federations in track and field, basketball, and gymnastics.

1972 The New York State Court of Appeals upholds the right of a New York City woman, Mrs. Bernice Gera, to be an umpire in professional baseball.

JANUARY 14

1882   The first United States country club, the Myopia Hunt Club of Winchester, Massachusetts, is formed.

1930   Bob Quinn, president of the Boston Red Sox, declared that no player connected with the Red Sox could enter the boxing ring after attempts were made to match Bill Barrett, Red Sox outfielder, with Arthur Shires, fighting first baseman of the Chicago White Sox.

1937   Sonny Siebert, baseball player, born.

1940   Baseball Commissioner Landis makes free agents of ninety-one players belonging to the Detroit club of the American League and fifteen farm affiliates on charges the clubs improperly handled players and engaged in wholesale covering up for Detroit.

1941   Ohio State University names Paul Brown whose Massillon High School teams lost one game in seven years to be its head football coach.

1942   Morris (Moe) Berg, Boston Red Sox catcher and a noted linguist, is granted an unconditional release by his club to accept a government appointment as a goodwill ambassador to Latin America.

1947   Gene A. Washington, football player, born.

1950   An unsuccessful attempt is made to expel seven schools including Villanova, Boston College, Maryland, Virginia, and The Citadel for violation of the NCAA "sanity code" against pay or special treatment for athletes.

1951   The first National Football League Pro Bowl All-Star game is held in Los Angeles, California with the American Conference defeating the National Conference 28-27.

1954   Joe DiMaggio married Marilyn Monroe.

1961   Federation Internationale de Skibob is founded in Innsbruck, Austria.

JANUARY 15

1882   The first American local ski club, the Nansen Ski Club of Berlin, New Hampshire, is formed.

1891   Raymond Chapman, the only player killed in a major league baseball game, in 1920, born.

1892   The basketball rules are published for the first time, in the *Triangle Magazine*, in Springfield, Massachusetts.

1892   Hobart (Hobey) Baker, hockey and football player, International Hockey Hall of Fame member, born.

1901   Luke Sewell, baseball player, manager, born.

1906   Willie Hoppe, the greatest billiard player of all time, wins the world billiard championship in Paris, France.

1911   Jerome Herman (Dizzy) Dean, baseball player, sports announcer, Baseball Hall of Fame member, born.

1920   Stephen Gromek, baseball player, born.

1920   Robert Davies, the National Basketball League's Most Valuable Player in the 1946-1947 season, Seton Hall College All-American in 1942 and 1943, born.

1930   Joe Grabowski, basketball player, born.

1941   The Cruising Club of America awards its Blue Water Medal to British yachtsmen for their part in the evacuation of Dunkerque.

1941   Jack Burke, Sr. wins the first Professional Golfers' Association Senior Championship held at Sarasota, Florida.

1943   Mike Marshall, baseball player, born.

1967   The first Super Bowl Game is held, at Los Angeles, California in the Coliseum, with the Green Bay Packers defeating the Kansas City Chiefs 35-10.

1968   Bill Masterson of the Minnesota North Stars died of brain injuries after being injured in a game against the Oakland Seals January 13th, the first death as a result of a game injury in National Hockey League history.

JANUARY 16

1866   The all metal screw clamp skate is patented by Everett Barney under Patent No. 52,301.

1870   Willie Simms, the Negro jockey who rode Ben Brush to victory in the 1896 Kentucky Derby, born.

1870   James Collins, manager of the 1903 American League Boston baseball team which won the first World Series, Baseball Hall of Fame member, born.

1891   The first American ski club association, the Central Organization, holds its first meeting and tournament at Ishpeming, Michigan.

1894   Berlin Guy Chamberlin, professional football coach, Professional Football Hall of Fame member, born.

1896   What is thought to be the first college basketball game with five players on a side takes place in Iowa City, Iowa between the University of Chicago and the University of Iowa with Chicago winning 15-12.

1897   Joseph Bodis, American Bowling Congress Hall of Fame member, born.

1935   A.J. Foyt, five times United States Automobile Club champion driver, born.

1936   The first electric eye photo finish camera at a race track is placed in operation at the Hialeah race track, at Hialeah, Florida.

1942   President Roosevelt tells his press conference that he favors the continuance of baseball if it can be done without interfering with war production or using healthy young men.

1960   The United States Lawn Tennis Association voted in favor of a proposal that up to thirteen open tournaments in which amateurs would compete against professionals be held throughout the world experimentally in 1961 under the auspices of the International Lawn Tennis Federaton.

1961   Mickey Mantle signs a $75,000 contract to become the highest paid baseball player in the American League.

1968   Baseball's 1967 American League champion, the Boston Red Sox, were named the 1967 Sports Team of the Year in an annual Associated Press poll of sportswriters and broadcasters.

1970   The owners of thirteen National Football League teams agree to a plan to split the League into three divisions.

1970   Curt Flood, former outfielder for the St. Louis Cardinals, files suit in federal court charging baseball with violation of the antitrust laws.

1973   Philadelphia Phillies pitcher Steve Carlton signs a one-year contract for a reported $167,000 making him the highest paid pitcher in baseball.

JANUARY 17

1795   The oldest curling club in existance, the Dudingston Curling Society, is organized in Edinburgh, Scotland.

1837   William Curtis, father of American rowing and American amateurism in sports, born.

1901   Joseph Bach, Notre Dame football tackle who played in front of the "Four Horsemen," born.

1901   Olin Dutra, golfer, PGA winner in 1932, United States Open winner in 1934, born.

1911   Harvey (Busher) Jackson, hockey player, Hockey Hall of Fame member, born.

1916   The Professional Golfers' Association of America is formed in New York.

1929   Jacques Plante, hockey player, Hart Trophy winner in 1962 as the National Hockey League Most Valuable Player, Vezina Trophy winner in 1962 as its leading goalie, born.

1945   Gilbert Dodds, holder of the indoor record for the mile, informs the National Amateur Athletic Union officials in New York that he is retiring from competition to assume full time gospel work.

1951   New York's third basketball scandal in five years occurs with the arrest of the two co-captains of Manhattan College's 1949-1950 team and three gamblers on bribery charges.

1968   Among the rule changes made by the NCAA's Football Rules Committee is the elimination of tackles as eligible pass receivers.

JANUARY 18

1886   The formation in England of the Hockey Association and of the striking circle is considered the birthday of modern field hockey.

1932   Joe Schmidt, football coach, born.

1938   Curtis Flood, baseball player, born.

1939   The Edward J. Neil Memorial Trophy awarded to the person who had done the most for boxing in the preceding year is awarded for the first time with the award going to Jack Dempsey.

1941   The Yale Scholarship Committee disclosed half the Yale varsity football squad in 1940 had received financial aid even though football supposedly was de-emphasized at Yale.

1941 It is revealed that Epinard, one of the great race horses of his generation, was found by Paris police being used as a delivery wagon horse after being stolen during the German occupation of France.

1942 Muhammad Ali, formerly Cassius Clay, heavyweight boxing champion of the world, born.

1944 Carl Morton, baseball player, National League Rookie of the Year in 1970, born.

1967 Barney Ross, world lightweight and welterweight boxing champion, died.

1967 Reese (Goose) Tatum, known as the "Clown Prince of Basketball" while playing with the Harlem Globetrotters, died.

JANUARY 19

1880 William Muldoon, the most famous nineteenth century wrestler in America, wins the Greco-Roman wrestling championship of America by defeating Thiebaud Bauer.

1886 The first active American local ski club, the Aurora Ski Club of Red Wing, Minnesota, was organized.

1888 Charles (Chick) Gandil, one of eight Chicago White Sox players banned from baseball for allegedly accepting bribes to throw the 1919 World Series, born.

1928 The first United States women's squash racquets singles championship is won by Eleanora Sears at the Round Hill Club, Greenwhich, Connecticut.

1942 The National Semi-Professional Baseball Congress reveals it may establish correspondence schools for baseball umpires to replace those drafted by the military.

1950 Jon Matlack, baseball player, 1972 National League Rookie of the Year, born.

1952 The Professional Golfers' Association tournament committee voted to modify a rule against Negro entries in golf tournaments sanctioned by the PGA by deciding they could play if invited by local tournament sponsors.

1952 The National Football League bought the New York Yankees franchise for $300,000 and announced that the club would be assigned to Dallas.

1953 Jesse Owens, 1936 Olympic track star, is named the Illinois Athletic Commission secretary.

1957 Tenley Albright announces her retirement from championship figure skating competition to enter Harvard Medical School.

1963 General of the Army Douglas MacArthur announced that the AAU and the NCAA had agreed to a settlement of their two and a half year old dispute for control of amateur sports in the United States.

1964 Frank Gifford plays for the East team in his eighth appearance in the professional football All-Star game.

1968 The Cleveland Indians and radio station WERE fired baseball announcer Jimmy Dudley who had been with the team since 1948.

JANUARY 20

1892   Students at the International YMCA Training School in Springfield, Massachusetts play the first official basketball game.

1928   Lionel Hebert, golfer, 1957 PGA championship winner, born.

1934   Camilo Pascual, baseball player, born.

1937   Bailey Howell, basketball player, born.

1940   Carol Heiss, Olympic women's singles figure skating champion in 1960, born.

1942   The Amateur Athletic Union announces plans for broadening of its competitive program to provide instruction and competition at various camps, forts, and naval stations to both train and entertain members of the armed forces, and to bring non-military citizens into the sports fields to better fit them for future call to the services.

1944   Elimination of the farm system would ruin baseball and eventually leave only those major league clubs with unlimited bankrolls in operation, warned Sam Breadon, president of the St. Louis Cardinals.

1951   Don Gehrmann wins his thirty-fifth consecutive victory winning the Knights of Columbus mile in Boston, Massachusetts in 4 minutes, 11.5 seconds, beating for the fourth time his arch rival, Fred Wilt.

1952   Patricia McCormick, the first professional American woman bull fighter, makes her professional debut in Ciudad Juarez, Mexico.

JANUARY 21

1879   Gilmour Dobie, football player, coach, Helms Hall of Fame member, born.

1884   Katie Sandwina, 6 foot, 1 inch tall, 220 pound woman weightlifter who reputedly once shouldered a 1,200 pound cannon, born.

1888   The Amateur Athletic Union of the United States is formed.

1922   Organizational meeting of the United States Field Hockey Association, the guiding organization for women's field hockey in the United States.

1922   The first slalom event in the sport of skiing is run at Murren, Switzerland.

1938   Dr. Marcus Hobart, Northwestern University team physician, says experiments at Northwestern disclose the new streamlined basketball rules eliminating the center jump after each field goal stimulates the hearts of players to a dangerous degree increasing the normal beat of 60 to 90 per minute in some cases up to 144.

1940   Jack Nicklaus, champion golfer, PGA Player of the Year in 1967, born.

1951   Mildred (Babe) Zaharias wins the Tampa Women's Open golf tournament and her total score of 288 sets a new women's golfing record for seventy-two holes medal play.

1957   Mickey Mantle received the Hickok Belt as the outstanding professional athlete in 1956.

1963   The 1940 Chicago Bears of the National Football League are named professional football's best all-time team in a poll of sports editors.

JANUARY 22

1915 W.R. (Bill) Durnan, hockey player, Vezina Trophy winner six times, Hockey Hall of Fame member, born.

1918 Elmer Lach, hockey player, Ross and Hart Trophy winner, Hockey Hall of Fame member, born.

1931 Galina Zybina, Russian athlete who ruled the female shot-putters for years, the first woman to achieve 50 feet in the shot-put, born.

1942 President Alva Bradley of the Cleveland Indians warned that night baseball could be turned into a carnival if overdone and hoped the owners would investigate thoroughly the wisdom of extending the present limit of seven home night games.

1942 Babe Didriksen Zaharias, Olympic Games track champion, announces her new goal of winning the national championship in both golf and tennis after being given full amateur status by the National Golf Association.

1951 Phil Rizzuto, New York Yankee shortstop, wins the first annual Ray Hickok professional athlete of the year award with the prize being a $10,000 belt.

1960 Paul Pender defeats Sugar Ray Robinson in a fifteen round split decision to gain world recognition as middleweight boxing champion.

1961 Wilma Rudolph sets a women's 60-yard dash world indoor record of 6.9 seconds, Ralph Bosten sets a world indoor broad jump record of 25 feet, 10 inches, and Parry O'Brien sets a shot-put world indoor record of 63 feet, 1 1/2 inches in a Los Angeles, California track meet.

1962 Jackie Robinson and Bob Feller are elected to the Baseball Hall of Fame and with his election Robinson becomes the first Negro to receive this honor.

1968 Duke Paoa Kahanamoku, Hawaiian Olympic swimming champion, died.

1973 George Foreman defeats Joe Frazier to become the world heavyweight boxing champion.

JANUARY 23

1879 The National Archery Association is formed at Crawfordsville, Indiana.

1893 A hundred mile skating race is held in Stamford, Connecticut and is won by Joe Donoghue in a time of 7 hours, 11 minutes, 38.2 seconds.

1923 Horace (Nip) Ashenfelter, 1952 Olympic gold medal winner in the 3,000-meter steeplechase, 1952 James E. Sullivan Memorial Trophy winner, 1952 Helms World Trophy selection for North America, born.

1930 Franklin Sullivan, baseball player, born.

1933 At the annual meeting of the Pacific Coast League, a minimum price of 25¢ for the bleachers and 40¢ for the grandstand was adopted for the 1933 baseball season.

1936 Jerry Kramer, football player, born.

1947   The National Football League empowers Commissioner Bert Bell to expel players involved in game fixing.

1949   Patty Berg ties the women's competitive seventy-two medal play record of 295 strokes in winning the Tampa Women's Open golf tournament.

1954   The United States Golf Association establishes an annual Bob Jones Award for sportsmanship in golf.

1957   Tom (Silent Tom) Smith, horse trainer, developer of Seabiscuit, died.

1964   Left-handed pitcher Warren Spahn of the National League Milwaukee Braves signs his contract for an estimated $85,000, the highest salary for a pitcher in baseball.

1971   Bob Cousy, Bob Pettit and Abe Saperstein are elected to the National Basketball Hall of Fame in Springfield, Massachusetts.

JANUARY 24

1870   William Morgan, inventor in 1895 of the sport of volleyball, born.

1930   Primo Carnera makes his American ring debut before 20,000 in New York knocking out Big Boy Peterson of Minneapolis in 1 minute, 10 seconds of the first round.

1944   Bobby Lee Bryant, football player, born.

1946   Capt. Tom Hamilton, developer of the wartime naval athletic program, is announced as the recipient of the New York Touchdown Club award for 1945 for his contribution to the advancement of football and for efforts to keep college football alive during the war by encouraging Navy trainees attending college to play intercollegiate football.

1947   Bill Bradley, football player, born.

1955   Baseball's rules committee, in an attempt to speed up games, announced strict enforcement for the 1955 season of the 20-second rule requiring a pitcher to deliver the ball within 20-seconds after he takes his pitching position providing the bases are unoccupied.

1964   Willie Shoemaker rides four winners at Santa Anita race track in Arcadia, California to up his career earnings of his horses to a record $30,040,005 topping the previous record of Eddie Arcaro.

1964   The Columbia Broadcasting System acquires network television rights to the National Football League regular season games in 1964 and 1965 for $14.1 million per year.

1969   Tom Zachary, the Washington Senators pitcher who threw the ball that became Babe Ruth's sixtieth home run in 1927, died.

JANUARY 25

1883   David (AB) Jenkins, auto racer, one of the first to begin speed runs on the Bonneville Salt Flats in Utah, born.

1924   Lou Groza, football player who scored 1,608 points in his twenty-one years in professional football, 1954 National Football League *The Sporting News* Player of the Year, born.

1925   Gordon Soltau, football player, sportscaster, born.

1932   Stamp collectors from all sections of the United States attend the opening sale of the commemorative stamp in honor of the Olympic winter games and 400,000 of the two cent stamp are sold the first day, at Lake Placid, New York.

1937   Don Maynard, football player, born.

1940   Charles Bachman, Michigan State College football coach, denies accusations he had used coercion to force football prospects to abandon other college sports.

1944   Eugene Washington, football player, born.

1945   Wallace Bunker, baseball player, born.

1948   Ed Goodson, baseball player, born.

1955   United States Attorney General Herbert Brownell, Jr. recommends to Congress that it prohibit transmission of gambling information on horse and dog racing via interstate and foreign communication sources.

1956   The University of Oklahoma disclosed it had awarded eighty football scholarships in 1955 at an average cost of $746 per scholarship.

1963   North and South Korea agreed to form a joint team for the 1964 Olympic Games in Tokyo, Japan.

1968   Bob Seagren clears 17 feet, 4 1/4 inches in a new world record mark for the indoor pole vault, in the Millrose Games, in Madison Square Garden, New York.

1973   Warren Spahn is elected to the Baseball Hall of Fame.

JANUARY 26

1871   The Rugby Football Union is formed in London, England to draft rugby rules.

1907   Thomas Henry Cotton, the greatest British professional golfer, born.

1908   Percy Beard, at 6 feet, 4 inches, one of the tallest men ever seen in top high hurdles competition, three times American champion, born.

1913   James Thorpe confesses in a letter to James E. Sullivan, chairman of the Amateur Athletic Union, that he had played professional baseball in 1909 and 1910 thereby disqualifying himself for amateur competition and forcing him to return the prizes he had won in the 1912 Olympic Games in Stockholm, Sweden.

1945   The New York Yankees baseball team are sold to a syndicate headed by Lawrence McPhail for an estimated $2,800,000.

1951   Mel Ott and Jimmy Foxx are elected to the Baseball Hall of Fame.

1955   Joe DiMaggio is elected to the Baseball Hall of Fame.

1956   The Winter Olympics open at Cortina d'Ampezzo, Italy and the Russians compete in Winter Olympics for the first time.

1960   Danny Heater of Burnsville, West Virginia set a presumed

United States one game individual scoring record for high school basketball players scoring 135 points as his team defeated Widen, West Virginia 173-43.

1960   Pete Rozelle is elected National Football League Commissioner succeeding Bert Bell.

1960   Lamar Hunt of Dallas is named the first president of the American Football League.

1965   Harry Stuhldreher, football player, coach, quarterback of the Notre Dame "Four Horsemen," died.

1970   National Football League Commissioner Pete Rozelle announced a $124,000,000 four year television pact with the three major television networks for the rights to televise National Football League league games, pre-season games, playoff games, and the Super Bowl.

JANUARY 27

1894   The University of Chicago, the first college to play a full basketball schedule, plays its first basketball game defeating the Chicago Y.M.C.A. Training School 19-11, winding up the season with a six wins and one loss record.

1918   John (Jack) Westrope, national champion jockey in 1933 when he was only fifteen years old, born.

1927   Fletcher (Joe) Perry, football player, Professional Football Hall of Fame member, the first professional football player to gain 1,000 yards rushing in two consecutive seasons, in 1953-1954, born.

1927   Robert Borkowski, baseball player, born.

1932   Max Baer, California heavyweight boxer, says he had conquered his fear of killing another in the ring and will meet King Levinsky in New York on the 29th without thought of pulling his punches.

1934   George Follmer, auto racer, born.

1941   Ray Dumont, president of the National Semi-Pro Baseball Congress, said the Congress will attempt to bring its 65,000 sandlot teams under a nationwide contract system to prevent a player from jumping from one club to another without proper releases.

1944   Casey Stengel, manager of the Boston Braves since 1938, resigns to give the new management of the baseball club a free hand.

1947   Rocky Graziano, ranking middleweight title challenger, is subpoenaed to appear before a New York Grand Jury to tell what he knows about an alleged gambling syndicate attempt to pull a betting coup on one of his fights.

1948   The Italian weekly sports review *Forza Italia* reports a Catholic Olympics, the first of its kind, may be held in conjunction with the 1950 Holy Year inspired by Pope Pius' many references to sports as "one of the forms of bodily education."

1953   John Skiles, a government attorney, in testimony in Philadelphia in the anti-trust suit against the National Football League, said the public was entitled to all benefits which might result from open television and radio broadcasting of professional football.

1956   Mrs. Roxanne Anderson, newly appointed manager of the United States women's track and field team for the 1956 Olympics, stated that she did not think American girls were cream puffs and believed they would meet the challenge of Russia in the Melbourne Games.

1964 The Helms Athletic Foundation announced its selections of the world's outstanding amateur athletes in 1963, the winners including Brian Sternberg, the United States pole vault champion.

JANUARY 28

1808 Messenger, the first American trotting horse, is buried.

1891 Barney Sedran, at 5 feet, 4 inches one of the smallest to excel in professional basketball, Basketball Hall of Fame member, born.

1908 Pat Kennedy, basketball referee, Basketball Hall of Fame member, born.

1913 Swedish authorities in the field of sport express an opinion that Jim Thorpe is entitled to retain the prizes he won in the Olympic Games in 1912 as his status as an amateur was questioned too late for the prizes to be taken away from him.

1922 The National Football League franchise of George Halas for the Staley Athletic Club in Decatur, Illinois is transferred to Chicago and the team is re-named the Chicago Bears.

1928 James (Pete) Runnels, baseball player, American League batting champion in 1960, born.

1932 Parry O'Brien, the greatest name in the history of shot-putting, born.

1933 Helen Wills Moody, the world's greatest woman tennis player, defeats a man, Phil Neer, in a tennis match before 3,000 fans at the Palace of Fine Arts in San Francisco, California but sportswriters claim Mrs. Moody was not tested by a good male tennis player.

1934 William White, baseball player, born.

1937 Charles Krueger, football player, born.

1943 Donald Hutson, star Green Bay Packer end who had been playing football for fourteen years, National Football League Most Valuable Player and two time Joe F. Carr award winner, retires.

1957 Emmett Kelly, formerly star clown of the Ringling Brothers, Barnum and Bailey Circus is signed by the Brooklyn Dodgers to entertain at ball games.

1958 Roy Campanella, one of baseball's greatest players, is seriously injured in an auto accident in New York and his playing career is ended.

1960 The National Football League votes to admit the Dallas Rangers team as a Western Conference member for the 1960 season.

1961 Valeri Brumel of the Soviet Union breaks the world indoor high jump record making 7 feet, 4 1/2 inches at a meet in Leningrad in Russia.

1965 Hungary's European middleweight champion, Laszlo Papp, announced that the Hungarian government's Supreme Sports Body had ordered him to quit professional boxing, a career labeled not compatible with socialist principles.

1967 Neal Steinhauer set a world indoor shot-put record of 67 feet, 10 inches in track and field competition at Portland, Oregon.

1970   Arthur Ashe, American Negro tennis star, is refused a visa by the South African government that he was trying to obtain in order to compete in the South African Open tennis championships.

1972   For the first time in the Monte Carlo automobile rally's sixty-one year history Italian drivers win the seven day, 2,300 mile event when Sandro Munari and Mario Manucci, driving a Lancia Fulvia, win.

1973   Typecast, a seven year old mare, is sold at public auction for $725,000, a new world record for a thoroughbred horse sold at public auction, at Inglewood, California.

JANUARY 29

1878   Berna (Barney) Oldfield, auto racer, first man to travel a mile a minute, in 1903, Auto Racing Hall of Fame member, born.

1884   John Schommer, basketball player, official, Basketball Hall of Fame member, born.

1892   Richard Norris Williams II, tennis champion, National Lawn Hal of Fame member, born.

1900   A new baseball league, the American League, is organized in Chicago, Illinois.

1900   Gus (Dynamite) Sonnenberg, called the "King of Wrestlers," the wrestler who introduced the flying tackle into wrestling, born.

1918   William Rigney, baseball player, manager, born.

1919   Henry (Hank) Edwards, baseball player, born.

1926   Bob Hollway, football coach, born.

1936   The first five members of the Baseball Hall of Fame are elected; Ty Cobb, Walter Johnson, Christy Mathewson, Babe Ruth, and Honus Wagner.

1939   Bobby Bolin, baseball player, born.

1963   Seventeen men were named as charter members of the Professional Football Hall of Fame at Canton, Ohio.

1964   The National Broadcasting Company wins television rights to the American Football League games for 1965-1969 on its $36,000,000 bid.

1967   The Veterans Committee of the Baseball Writers Association of America elects Branch Rickey and Lloyd (Little Poison) Waner to the Baseball Hall of Fame.

1967   Stien Kaiser of The Netherlands sets a world women's speed skating record for 3,000 meters of 5 minutes, 4.8 seconds, in Davos, Switzerland.

1968   Adolph Rupp became the biggest winning coach in basketball history when his team, the Kentucky Wildcats, wins a game against Mississippi giving him his 772nd victory.

JANUARY 30

1909   The Rocky Mountain Conference is organized under the name Colorado Faculty Athletic Conference.

1910   The first American board track automobile speedway, the Los Angeles Motordrome, is started near Playa del Rey, California.

1917   Therman Gibson, American Bowling Congress Hall of Fame member, born.

1922   Professional football gets its first eight column newspaper headline, "Stagg says Conference will break professional football menace," in the Chicago *Herald and Examiner*.

1923   Walter Dropo, baseball player, American League Rookie of the Year in 1950, born.

1933   The depression forces the University of California at Los Angeles to trim minor sports budgets and to entirely eliminate baseball as a subsidized activity.

1941   Paul Flatley, football player, National Football League Rookie of the Year in 1963 by *The Sporting News*, born.

1942   Mrs. Hranoush Bey, known as Madame Bey to the boxing world, operator of a training camp near Summit, New Jersey, died.

1945   William Alexander, head football coach at Georgia Tech since 1920 retires, turning over his post to Bobby Dodds.

1949   In the annual Kendallville Screwball Golf Tournament at Kendallville, Indiana held for the benefit of the March of Dimes and played in subfreezing temperatures and snow, a record number of entries, 253, some in bathing suits, play a course spiked with unusual hazards such as innerspring mattresses and barrels, and Nap Chinick wins with a 43 stroke total for the nine holes.

1951   Jesse Hill, University of Southern California track coach and former major league baseball player, is named head football coach at the University of Southern California.

1960   Oakland is awarded the former Minneapolis franchise in the American Football League.

1960   Carol Heiss wins the women's singles United States figure skating championship in Seattle, Washington.

1960   John Thomas sets a world indoor high jump record of 7 feet, 1 1/2 inches in the Millrose Games in New York.

JANUARY 31

1893   George (Tioga) Burns, baseball player, American League Most Valuable Player selection by the League in 1926, born.

1913   Donald Hutson, football player, Professional Football Hall of Fame, Helms Hall of Fame member, leader of the National Football League eight years in pass receiving, five times National Football League scoring champion, born.

1914   Jersey Joe Walcott, the oldest fighter in modern ring history to win the heavyweight title winning it in 1951 at the age of thirty-seven, born.

1916   Frank Parker, tennis player who was ranked in the first ten for seventeen years from 1933 to 1949, born.

1919   Jackie Robinson, major league baseball's first Negro player, Baseball Hall of Fame member, born.

1931 Ernie Banks, baseball player, National League Most Valuable Player in 1958 and 1959, born.

1932 Henry Aguirre, baseball player, born.

1934 Before one of the largest crowds ever to see a wrestling match, 20,000, in Chicago, Illinois, Jim Londos, who claims the heavyweight wrestling title, wins over Joe Savoldi, a former Notre Dame fullback, in a one fall match.

1945 Five Brooklyn College basketball players admitted they had accepted a $1,000 bribe to throw a game with Akron University.

1947 Nolan Ryan, baseball player, born.

1948 Gilbert Dodds set a 4 minute, 5.3 seconds world indoor record for the mile at the Millrose Games in New York to retire the Wanamaker Trophy.

1950 Paul Pettit, lefthanded baseball player who pitched six no-hit games for a Lomita, California high school team, signed with the Pittsburgh Pirates for bonuses and guarantees of about $100,000, a record for bonuses.

1961 The 1960 World Series winners, the Pittsburgh Pirates, were chosen the athletic team of the year for 1960 in an Associated Press poll of writers and broadcasters with the National Football League professional champion Philadelphia Eagles second and the United States Olympic hockey team third in the balloting.

1967 Thirty-eight members of the Harness Tracks of America established a protective force similar to the Thoroughbred Racing Protective Bureau to control unlawful practices in their sport.

1972 Karl Schranz, Austrian downhill ski racer, is declared ineligible for the winter Olympic Games by the International Olympic Committee because of professional activities.

FEBRUARY 1

1908 Albert (Albie) Booth, one of Yale's greatest football players, National Football Foundation Hall of Fame member, born.

1929 In weightlifting, the first 400 pound clean and jerk is attributed to Charles Rigoulet of France who reaches 402 1/2 pounds.

1938 Jacky Cupit, golfer, *Golf Digest's* Rookie of the Year for 1961, born.

1949 Barbara Ann Scott, Olympic and world figure skating champion is named the winner of the Lou E. Marsh Memorial Trophy as Canada's outstanding athlete of 1948 in a Canadian Press poll.

1949 Louis B. Mayer sold his race horse breeding farm near Los Angeles, California for an estimated $1,000,000.

1950 Earl (Curley) Lambeau, Green Bay Packer football coach for thirty-one years, switches to the Chicago Cardinals as coach and vice-president.

1956 Soviet Communist youth weekly *Komsomolsakya Pravda* rebuked Soviet colleges for overemphasizing championship and record breaking athletes at the expense of physical education of all students.

1968 Lawson Little, winner in 1934 and 1935 of both the British and United States amateur golf championships, died.

1971 Brooks Robinson of the Baltimore Orioles baseball team is named the winner of the Hickok Professional Athlete of the Year award finishing ahead of George Blanda and Bobby Orr in the polling.

FEBRUARY 2

1876 Eight baseball teams band together to form the National League.

1881 Karl Frederick, 1920 Olympic champion for the 50-meter pistol event, born.

1889 The United States National Lawn Tennis Association issues a statement extending its protective wing to "lady Lawn Tennis" players.

1891 Frank Foyston, hockey player, a member of the 1917 Seattle club, the first United States based team ever to win a Stanley Cup, Hockey Hall of Fame member, born.

1895 George Halas, owner of the Chicago Bears, football pioneer, born.

1908 Clarence (Buster) Crabbe, Olympic gold medal winner in 1932 in the 400-meter swimming competition, movie star, born.

1913 Jim Thorpe signs with the New York Giants to play professional baseball.

1918 John L. Sullivan, heavyweight boxing champion of the world, died.

1923 Albert (Red) Schoendienst, baseball player, manager, set a National League record for second baseman in 1949 for handling the ball 320 consecutive plays without an error, born.

1934 Gene Tunney, former world heavyweight champion, was reported to be marshalling political support to run for Congress on the Democratic ticket from the Fourth District in Connecticut.

1949 Ben Hogan, golfing champion, is seriously injured in a car accident in Van Horn, Texas.

1957 Tommy Kono, light heavyweight weightlifter, sets a world record of 989 pounds, in Honolulu, Hawaii.

1959 Vince Lombardi signed a five year contract as head coach and general manager of the National Football League's Green Bay Packers.

1960 John DeJohn and Joe Netro, co-managers of ex-world welterweight and middleweight champion Carmen Basilio, are barred for life from boxing activities in New York by the New York State Athletic Commission for illegal payments to Gabe Genovese, an unlicensed ex-promoter, matchmaker, and manager.

1962 John Uelses became the first man to pole vault 16 feet by clearing 16 feet, 1/4 inch at the Millrose Games in New York.

1967 Formation of the second professional basketball league, the American Basketball Association, is announced.

1970 Pete Maravich of Louisiana State University becomes the first collegiate basketball player in history to shatter 3,000 points when he tallies 49 points in a game against Mississippi State.

FEBRUARY 3

1899 Forrest (Red) DeBernardi, basketball player, Basketball Hall of Fame member, born.

1922 James Robert Dyck, baseball player, born.

1926 Arthur Arfons, auto racer, racing car designer, born.

1931 Jim Corbett, former heavyweight champion, in Los Angeles, states that boxing in the United States will never be restored to its former prestige until state boxing commissions are abolished and a national commission with unlimited regulatory powers is created.

1938 Lou Boudreau, captain of the University of Illinois basketball team and a star baseball player, was suspended from the Illinois basketball team for receiving, allegedly, monthly checks from the Cleveland baseball club of the American League.

1939 Charles (Cash and Carry) Pyle, the P.T. Barnum of sports promoting, the sponsor of the Bunion Derby, and the professional tours of Red Grange and Suzanne Lenglen, died.

1940 Francis (Fran) Tarkenton, football player, born.

1941 Carol Mann, golfer, 1965 United States Women's Open winner, born.

1945 Robert Griese, football player, *The Sporting News* American Football Conference Player of the Year in 1971, born.

1947 Joe Coleman, baseball player, born.

1951 The Southern Conference decides to use freshman on all varsity sports teams.

1951 Dick Button wins the United States figure skating title for the sixth time.

1961 Manhattan College's four man relay team ran the two mile relay in world indoor record time of 7 minutes, 32.8 seconds at the Millrose Games in New York.

1962 The United States Lawn Tennis Association votes at its annual meeting for national control of open tournaments and against elimination of distinctions between amateurs and professionals.

1964 The University of Kentucky basketball team defeats Georgia 108-83 giving Coach Adolf Rupp his 700th victory in thirty-three seasons.

1964 Tom O'Hara sets a world indoor mile record of 3 minutes, 56.6 seconds in winning the Baxter Mile at the New York Athletic Club meet in New York.

1972 The first Winter Olympics in Asia opens at Sapporo, Japan.

FEBRUARY 4

1912 Byron Nelson, golfer, Athlete of the Year in 1944, winner of nineteen golf tournaments in 1945, born.

1913 Woody Hayes, football coach, College Football Coach of the Year in 1968, born.

1929 Neil Johnston, basketball player, born.

1931 Baseball's drive to take the hop from the rabbit ball is one reason for the adoption of a new style official ball by the National League with a heavier and looser cover and heavier and more perma-

29

nent stitching enabling pitchers to get a better grip and reducing the resiliency of the ball on ground hits.

1932 The first American Winter Olympic Games begins at Lake Placid, New York.

1939 Glenn Cunningham, the world record holder for the mile, says that he agrees with Brutus Hamilton, the track coach of the University of California, that the four minute mile is beyond human effort and the best a man could run would be 4 minutes, 1.66 seconds.

1952 Jackie Robinson of the Brooklyn Dodgers became the first Negro executive of a major radio or television network when he was named director of communication activities for NBC's New York stations.

1962 In *Nedelya*, the weekly supplement to the Soviet paper *Izvestia*, it is claimed that baseball is "Beizbol," an old Russian game.

1965 Greyhound, world champion trotter, dies at the age of thirty-three.

1971 Bowie Kuhn, baseball commissioner, announced a separate section of the Baseball Hall of Fame honoring Black players of the pre-integration era before 1947.

FEBRUARY 5

1875 First issue of *The Kentucky Live Stock Record* covering all breeds of livestock which in 1891 changed its name to *The Thoroughbred Record* and devoted itself strictly to thoroughbred race horses.

1903 Joan Whitney Payson, co-owner of Greentree Stable, one of America's foremost thoroughbred breeders and racing stables, and owner of the New York Mets baseball team, born.

1934 Henry (Hank) Aaron, baseball player, 1957 National League Most Valuable Player, National League home run leader many times, born.

1934 Abraham Woodson, football player, born.

1942 Roger Staubach, football player, Heisman Trophy winner in 1963, *The Sporting News* National Football Conference Player of the Year in 1971, born.

1943 Craig Morton, football player, born.

1948 Richard Button becomes the first American Olympic figure skating champion.

1948 Gretchen Fraser becomes the first American woman slalom Olympic champion winning a silver medal in the Alpine combination at St. Moritz, Switzerland.

1949 The official Federation Equestre Internationale equestrian high jump record is 8 feet, 1 1/4 inches performed by a horse named Huaso ridden by Capt. Larraguibel Morales of Chile, at Santiago, Chile.

1956 Bill Mihalo of Hollywood, California set a world professional record of 2 hours, 28 minutes, 1 second for the twenty mile walk, in San Fernando, California.

1972 Bob Douglas, owner and coach of the Renaissance Five, becomes the first Negro ever to be honored for individual achievements in basketball when he is elected to the Basketball Hall of Fame.

FEBRUARY 6

1895   George (Babe) Ruth born.
1926   Richard Long, baseball player, born.
1926   A rule is adopted making all players ineligible for National Football League competition until after their college classes graduate.
1927   Forrest (Smokey) Burgess, baseball player, born.
1929   Sixten Jernberg, skier, winner of four golds, three silver, and two bronze medals in Olympic skiing, born.
1932   The first dog sled race on an Olympic demonstration program begins, at Lake Placid, New York.
1943   The Office of Defense Transportation asks that the 1943 Kentucky Derby be canceled because of transportation difficulties.
1947   Charles Hickcox, winner of three gold medals and a silver medal in swimming events in the 1968 Olympic Games, born.
1948   Barbara Ann Scott of Canada won the Olympic women's figure skating title.
1955   President Eisenhower is cited by the Golf Writers Association of America as the person making the outstanding contribution to golf in 1954.
1956   Professional golfer Cary Middlecoff speaking in Dallas, Texas states he once had been offered a bribe to lose a minor tournament and expressed concern that easy money times and gambling might cause a golf scandal similar to ones which had been suffered by basketball.
1960   John Thomas equals his world indoor high jump record of 7 feet, 1 1/2 inches in a Boston, Massachusetts track meet.
1968   Joan Whitney Payson is elected president of the New York Mets baseball team.

FEBRUARY 7

1935   Gene Sarazen, former national and British Open golf champion, refuses to play in the Caliente golf tournament in Mexico because of the pari-mutuel system of wagering on the players.
1941   The University of Southern California basketball team defeated UCLA 43-41 in Los Angeles although Jackie Robinson, Bruin forward, scores twenty points for the losers, and by losing this game UCLA had lost every basketball meeting with USC since 1932, thirty-four straight games.
1942   Cornelius Warmerdam clears 15 feet, 3/8 inches to become the first man ever to achieve a fifteen foot pole vault jump indoors.
1947   Jimmy Demaret equals the all time competitive golf record in a PGA sponsored event with a 62, in the first round of the Texas Open golf tournament at San Antonio, Texas.
1964   Art Rooney, founder and owner of the Pittsburgh Steelers, is elected to the Professional Football Hall of Fame.
1969   At Hialeah race track in Miami, Florida, Diane Crump became the first woman jockey to ride at a United States pari-mutuel track but finished tenth in a field of twelve horses.

1973   Monte Irvin is elected to the Baseball Hall of Fame by the Special Committee of the Negro Leagues, the fourth player selected since the committee was created in 1971 to open the Hall of Fame to the heroes of Black baseball.

FEBRUARY 8

1887   The Aurora Ski Club, the first active American local ski club, holds its first skiing competition in Red Wing, Minnesota.

1896   Faculty representatives of universities of the Middle West meet and form the Western (Big Ten) Conference.

1921   Walter Arthur (Hoot) Evers, baseball player, born.

1921   Willard Warren Marshall, baseball player, born.

1932   Before one of the largest boxing crowds in Milwaukee in twenty-five years, 8,050 paid admissions, Jack Dempsey defeats two opponents, Buck Everett and Jack Roper, in a pair of exhibition two round bouts.

1936   Jay Berwanger becomes the first player selected in the first National Football League draft when he is chosen by the Philadelphia team.

1937   Cletis Boyer, baseball player, born.

1939   Glenn Cunningham, the Kansas miler, requested that track and field fans planning to attend the Pennsylvania Athletic Club indoor meet at Philadelphia refrain from smoking since the less smoke in the arena the better the winning time.

1939   Miss June Bierbower, sports editor of the student publication *The Daily Nebraskan* of the University of Nebraska, said she expected to get along in what was a man's field noting she could always send someone to invade the dressing rooms.

1941   The United States Lawn Tennis Association adopts regulations barring tennis players from the payrolls of sporting goods manufacturers.

1943   Bob Oliver, baseball player, born.

1957   Ira Murchison tied the world indoor record of 6.1 seconds for the 60-yard dash in the Michigan Amateur Athletic Union relays in Ann Arbor, Michigan.

FEBRUARY 9

1887   Henry (Heinie) Zimmerman, baseball player, the 1912 National League batting champion with a .372 average and its home run leader with 14, born.

1895   The first basketball game between two colleges takes place as Minnesota State School of Agriculture defeats Hamline College 9-3.

1907   Aubrey (Dit) Clapper, hockey player, Hockey Hall of Fame member, a member of the Boston Bruins hockey team for twenty years, born.

1914   William Veeck, baseball club owner, born.

1931   Helene Madison, ranked as the greatest woman swimmer of all time, is reported by her father to have refused offers amounting to $17,500 to turn professional.

1932   The first American two man bob sled competition begins at Lake Placid, New York as part of the Olympic Winter Games.

1942   The Philadelphia National League baseball club lists its nickname as the "Phils" instead of the "Phillies" used by the team since the 1880s because "Phillies" was being used by a nationally advertised commercial product.

1958   John Devitt, Gary Chapman, Jon Konrads, and Geoff Shipton of Australia swim the 440-yard freestyle relay in world record time of 3 minutes, 47.3 seconds in Sydney, Australia.

1960   A no tampering verbal pact is announced between the American Football League and the National Football League as to player contracts.

1963   Valeri Brumel is defeated by John Thomas in the high jump for the first time, both clearing 7 feet, 1/4 inches but Thomas being the winner because of fewer misses.

FEBRUARY 10

1893   William Tilden, the first American to win the Wimbledon men's singles tennis title, born.

1905   Walter Brown, a major force in organizing the National Basketball Association, born.

1906   John (Cat) Thompson, basketball player, Basketball Hall of Fame member, born.

1919   Allie Reynolds, baseball player, leading pitcher in the American League in 1952 with a 2.07 earned run average, born.

1920   The joint rules committee of baseball's National and American Leagues outlaws all pitches that involved tampering with the ball, including application of sandpaper or emery paper to the ball.

1932   The first international ski meet of importance in the United States begins at Lake Placid, New York as part of the Olympic winter games.

1950   Mark Spitz, winner of seven gold medals in swimming at the 1972 Olympics, a record for one performer at a single Olympic Games, born.

1951   Don Gehrmann beat Fred Wilt in the Baxter Mile in New York in a time of 4 minutes, 8.2 seconds to gain permanent possession of the Baxter Cup.

1953   Members of the Laborite opposition in the Irish parliament criticize Premier Eamon de Valera's regime for spending $700,000 to buy the 1952 English Derby winner Tulyar for the government sponsored Irish National Stud.

1954   Eastern (Ivy) League colleges adopted a rule requiring each member play the other seven Ivy League schools at football every season.

1962   Jim Beatty, the first American to run an indoor mile in less than 4 minutes, accomplishes the feat in 3 minutes, 58.9 seconds, in Los Angeles, California.

FEBRUARY 11

1878   The Boston Bicycle Club, the first American bicycle club, is formed in Boston.

1900   Thomas (Tommy) Hitchcock, Jr., the Babe Ruth of polo, born.

1909   Max Baer, heavyweight boxing champion of the world, born.

1924   Harold Rice, baseball player, born.

1938   The Hollywood Turf Club in Inglewood, California announces it will prohibit pari-mutuel betting on horses entered in races strictly for tune up purposes for other events in its summer meeting by asking owners to declare in advance whether he plans to let the horse run or merely to give him an easy race.

1949   Willie Pep regains the world featherweight boxing title by defeating Sandy Saddler in New York.

1957   The National Hockey League Players Association is formed in New York.

1962   At the Daytona Speedway at Daytona Beach, Florida, the world's best drivers — from stock car to grand prix — compete for the first time in auto racing history with the winner being Dan Gurney in a Lotus sports car.

1968   The 20,000 seat sports arena at the new Madison Square Garden in New York is officially opened.

1973   Shane Gould set a world swimming record of 16 minutes, 56.9 seconds for the 1,500-meter freestyle, the first woman to finish the distance in under 17 seconds.

FEBRUARY 12

1831   John Morrissey, the boxer who helped develop Saratoga Springs, New York as a racing resort, born.

1878   Frederick Thayer patents the baseball catcher's mask under Patent No. 200,358.

1880   The National Croquet League is organized in Philadelphia.

1889   Harold (Curly) Byrd, one of the few football coaches to be a university president, becoming president of the University of Maryland, born.

1896   Isaac Murphy, the Negro jockey who won three Kentucky Derby races, died.

1908   Start of the New York to Paris automobile race.

1918   Dominic DiMaggio, baseball player, born.

1926   Joe Garagiola, baseball player, sports broadcaster, born.

1934 Bill Russell, basketball player, the 1955 and 1956 College Basketball Player of the Year, five time winner of the Podoloff Cup for professional basketball, born.

1937 Charles Dumas, the 1956 Olympic gold medal winner in the high jump, born.

1942 Leslie MacMitchel of New York University wins the mile run at the Metropolitan intercollegiate championships in New York in 4 minutes, 8 seconds, the fastest ever run in college competition indoors or out.

1944 Charles Pasarell, tennis player, the 1966 and 1967 men's indoor singles champion and the 1966 national intercollegiate champion, born.

1954 Pierre Etchebaster, world open court tennis champion since 1928, announces his retirement at the age of sixty.

FEBRUARY 13

1883 Harold (Hal) Chase, baseball player, manager, born.

1912 Jose de Capriles, member of the 1936, 1948, and 1952 American fencing teams in the Olympics, born.

1918 Patty Berg, golfer, three times Associated Press Woman Athlete of the Year, winner of more than eighty tournaments, born.

1920 The National Negro Baseball League is organized.

1922 Peter Paul Castiglione, baseball player, born.

1930 Stella Walsh, a seventeen year old girl from Cleveland, Ohio, sets her second world's record in a week winning the 220-yard international girls sprint at the Meadowbrook Games in Philadelphia in a time of 26 4/5 seconds.

1931 The director of athletics at the United States Naval Academy calls for a Navy home football stadium in Washington, D.C. as part of the program to beautify the city and because the Navy had never been allowed to charge admission for its home games at its 25,000 capacity stadium at Annapolis, Maryland.

1944 Sal Bando, baseball player, born.

1953 Senator Edwin Johnson warns baseball's major leagues that Congress would not stand for them destroying minor league baseball by nationwide telecasts such as a proposed baseball game of the week program.

1956 Auburn was placed on indefinite probation and barred from post season football games by the Southeastern Conference for having paid Harry and Robert Beaube, high school football players from Gadsden, Alabama, $500 each to enroll at Auburn.

1963 Harry Steers, bowler, charter member of Bowling's Hall of Fame, died.

1965 Sixteen year old Peggy Fleming wins the United States ladies senior figure skating title at Lake Placid, New York.

1973 Mrs. Augustus Riggs 4th, only the fourth best-in-show woman judge in the history of the Westminster Kennel Club Show in New York, names Ch. Acadia Command Performance, a white standard poodle, the best in show.

FEBRUARY 14

1907   The Masters of the Fox Hounds Association, the first American fox hound association, is formed in New York.

1910   John Longden, jockey, trainer, rider of Count Fleet in his Triple Crown victories, born.

1913   Mel Allen, sports broadcaster, born.

1923   Jay Hebert, golfer, 1960 PGA title winner, with his brother Lionel named the 1967 Golfing Family of the Year award winner, born.

1931   Bernie (Boom Boom) Geoffrion, Canadian hockey player, 1961 Hart Trophy and Art Ross Trophy winner, born.

1935   Mary (Mickey) Wright, Woman Athlete of the Year in 1963, four time winner of the United States women's open golf championship, born.

1941   Frank Leahy is named head football coach of Notre Dame.

1942   Cornelius Warmerdan sets a new world record for the pole vault of 15 feet, 7 1/4 inches, the fifteenth time he had vaulted 15 feet or better.

1943   Berlin radio reports Reich Sports Leader Hans von Tschammer und Osten has banned all but local athletic competition.

1951   Sugar Ray Robinson wins the world middleweight title defeating Jake LaMotta in Chicago, Illinois, the first time a welterweight champion dethroned a middleweight title holder and Robinson's fifth decision over LaMotta in six fights.

1966   Wilt Chamberlain of the Philadelphia 76ers set a National Basketball Association career scoring record of 20,884 points, in seven seasons of play, in a game in Charleston, West Virginia.

FEBRUARY 15

1897   Earl Blaik, football coach, College Football Coach of the Year in 1946, born.

1905   The first racing meet at the present Oaklawn Park, Hot Srings, Arkansas, opens.

1929   Graham Hill, auto racer, winner of the international auto racing championship in 1962 and 1968, born.

1940   John Hadl, football player, in 1967 tied the American Football League record for the most consecutive games — nineteen — for throwing a touchdown pass, born.

1946   The Philadelphia Phillies hire Edith Houghton, a thirty-three year old discharged WAVE and former star girl baseball player as a baseball scout.

1950   A nationwide poll of sportswriters and sportscasters completes reporting Associated Press' top competitors and events of the past fifty years with the top competitors including such athletes as Jim Thorpe, Babe Ruth, George Mikan, Jack Dempsey, Bobby Jones, Man o'War, Johnny Weismuller, Bill Tilden, Jesse Owens, and Mildred (Babe) Zaharias.

1953   Tenley Albright becomes the first American woman world figure skating champion winning the title at Davos, Switzerland.

1956 John Haines ties the world indoor record of 6.1 seconds for the 60-yard dash in a track meet in Lawrenceville, New Jersey.

1962 CBS contracted in New York to pay the National Collegiate Athletic Association $10,200,000 during the next two years for exclusive rights to televise NCAA football games, the highest fee so far for a sports package on a per year basis.

1970 Billy Kidd of Vermont wins the men's combined title in the Alpine World Ski Championship at Val Gardena, Italy, the first United States world title in the Alpine combination.

FEBRUARY 16

1858 Laurence (Lon) Myers who at one time held all the United States track records for all distances from fifty yards to a mile is born.

1866 William (Sliding Billy) Hamilton, baseball player, Baseball Hall of Fame member, born.

1926 Suzanne Lenglen remains undisputed women's tennis champion of the world by defeating Helen Wills at Cannes, France in the only meeting between the two champions.

1934 Marlene Bauer Hagge, golfer, 1950 Woman Athlete of the Year, at eighteen the youngest winner of the Ladies Professional Golf Association championship title, born.

1942 Cornelius Warmerdam who made a record pole vault of 15 feet, 7 1/4 inches in the Boston A.A. games is voted unanimously all the first place ballots of the Boston sportswriters and receives the Hallahan Memorial Trophy, the second time he had received this Trophy by unanimous choice having previously been selected in 1939.

1943 Bobby Darwin, baseball player, born.

1952 De-emphasis of football and other intercollegiate sports including the banning of post-season games and aboliton of spring practice and outright athletic scholarships was urged in a report adopted by the Executive Committee of the American Council on Education.

1962 Jimmy Bostwick defeats his brother Pete Bostwick to win the United States Open court tennis championship for the third time.

1963 Mary Revell of Detroit, Michigan made the first recorded round trip swim across the Strait of Messina between Sicily and the Italian mainland.

1972 Wilt Chamberlain of the Los Angeles Lakers becomes the first player in the National Basketball Association to score 30,000 points finishing a game against the Phoenix Suns with 30,003 points, his total being achieved in 940 regular season games.

FEBRUARY 17

1892 Robert Neyland, runner-up in a poll of coaches during football's centennial year to Knute Rockne as the greatest college coach, born.

1908 Red Barber, sportscaster, born.

1924   Johnny Weissmuller swims the 100-yard freestyle in a world record time of 52 2/5 seconds, at Miami, Florida.

1936   Jim Brown, football player, Jim Thorpe Trophy winner for the most valuable National Football League player in 1958, 1963, and 1965, Professional Football Hall of Fame member, voted football back of the decade 1950-1960, born.

1949   Richard Button retains the men's figure skating world championship in competition in Paris, France.

1951   John Marshall swims the 500-meter freestyle in New Haven, Connecticut in world record time of 5 minutes, 43.7 seconds.

1951   In an effort to discourage off-track gambling, the Florida State Racing Commission rules that race results could not be transmitted by news services from Florida until twenty minutes after they are posted.

1955   Tenley Albright regains the world's women's figure skating championship in competition at Vienna, Austria.

1958   Frank Gifford, National Football League New York Giants halfback, signed a seven year film contract with Warner Brothers.

1964   Luke Appling is elected as the 101st member of the Baseball Hall of Fame.

1968   Mamie Rollins sets 70-yard low women's hurdles world record of 8.7 seconds.

1968   The Naismith Memorial Basketball Hall of Fame at Springfield College in Springfield, Massachusetts is opened.

FEBRUARY 18

1853   August Belmont, Jr., breeder of Man o'War and founder of the New York Jockey Club, born.

1895   George Gipp, Notre Dame football star, National Football Foundation Hall of Fame member, the first All-American from Notre Dame, born.

1922   Kenesaw Mountain Landis resigns from the bench as a United States District judge in Illinois to devote all his time to baseball.

1928   Jim McElreath, auto racer, 1970 Ontario 500 winner, born.

1932   Sonja Henie retains the world women's figure skating championship, the sixth time she had won the title, in Montreal, Canada.

1932   Mrs. Florence Wolf Dreyfuss is elected chairman of the board of directors of the Pittsburgh Pirates baseball team.

1938   Manuel (Geronimo) Mota, baseball player, born.

1941   Homer Jones, football player, born.

1950   John Mayberry, baseball player, born.

1967   Bob Seagren sets a world indoor pole vault record of 17 feet, 3 inches at the Knights of Columbus meet in Cleveland, Ohio.

1971   Ken Buchanan of Scotland, the lightweight champion of the world, is named winner of the Edward J. Neil Memorial Award as the top prizefighter of 1970.